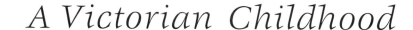

A Victorian Childhood

At Work

Ruth Thomson

W

FRANKLIN WATTS
LONDON • SYDNEY

First published in 2007 by Franklin Watts
338 Euston Road, London NW1 3BH

Franklin Watts Australia
Level 17/207 Kent Street
Sydney NSW 2000

Designer: Mei Lim
Editor: Susie Brooks

The author would like to thank John and Sandy Howarth of Swiss
Cottage Antiques, Leeds and Islington Education Library Service
(www.objectlessons.org) for the loan of items from their collection,
and Bella Bennett.

Photographic acknowledgements
Neil Thomson 7t, 9t, 10t, 10b, 11bl, 12t, 16br, 17bl, 18tr, 20t, 21b, 24,
27r, 28c, 28b; Peter Millard/Franklin Watts Picture Library 5b, Martin
Chillmaid/Franklin Watts Picture Library 11br, 14t; Ironbridge Gorge
Museum Trust 5t, 6b; Mary Evans Picture Library 13, 14b; London
Metropolitan Archives cover/c, 15, 19t, 25b.

A CIP catalogue record for this book is available
from the British Library.
Dewey Decimal Classification Number: 941.081

ISBN 978 0 7496 7050 4

Printed and bound in Malaysia

Franklin Watts is a division of Hachette Children's Books.

Contents

CHILD WORKERS

In early Victorian Britain, there was a huge difference between the way that rich and poor children lived.

What differences do you notice between these rich children and the poor ones below?

Rich children

Rich children lived in comfortable homes. They were warm, well dressed and had enough to eat. Boys went to school and girls were taught at home, but they both had plenty of spare time for playing.

Poor children

Poor children were not so lucky. Their parents sent them out to work as young as six, so that the family earned enough money for food. Children worked long hours, often in terrible conditions, in **textile** mills, down mines, in brickyards, on farms or selling things in the street.

These children are receiving pay for their tiring work carrying heavy loads of clay in a brickyard.

Young boys, known as nippers, worked as sweepers. They spent the day on all fours, brushing away fluff under fast-moving machinery.

Cotton mills

Cotton mill owners mainly employed women and children, because they did not have to pay them as much as men. Many of the children were **orphans**, who lived as well as worked at the mill. They worked for more than twelve hours a day, six days a week, every week of the year.

Full of danger

Cotton mills were unhealthy places to work. Windows were kept closed to prevent the thread from drying and snapping. Thick clouds of cotton dust made it hard to breathe. The machines had no guards, so children often had terrible accidents, getting limbs, hair or clothes caught in the whirling cogs and gears.

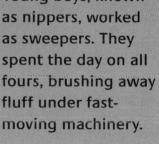

▲ Clogs worn by a child worker

NASTY JOBS

Early Victorians did not see anything wrong with children working. There were few **laws** controlling children's working hours or conditions.

The Earl of Shaftesbury ▶

Coal mines

Some of the worst places children worked were coal mines. The children developed twisted limbs from pushing the heavy coal wagons. They had breathing problems from the poisonous gases and dust they **inhaled**. Some died in explosions and accidents.

Studying children at work

Lord Ashley (who later became the Earl of Shaftesbury) persuaded **Parliament** to send **commissioners** to find out about children's work. They published reports which included interviews with children. The report on mines had drawings like this one below, which greatly shocked the public.

In mines, older children worked as 'putters'. They filled and pushed the coal wagons along rails to the mine shaft.

Younger children worked as 'trappers'. They sat for ten hours a day alone in dark, wet tunnels. They opened doors to let wagons through and to let fresh air into the mine.

▲ Chimney brush and poles

Ellison Jack an eleven-year-old girl coal-carrier interviewed for *The Report of the Commission of Mines 1842*

I have been working below three years on my father's account. He takes me down to the mine at 2 [*o'clock*] in the morning and I come up at 1 or 2 the next afternoon. I go to bed at 6 at night to be ready next morning. I have to bear my burden [*load of coal*] up four traps or ladders, before I get to the main road that leads to the pit bottom. My task is four to five tubs; each tub holding four-and-quarter hundredweight [*equal to 50 kilos*]. I fill five tubs in 20 journeys. I have had the strap [*been beaten*] when I did not do my bidding. I am glad when my task is wrought [*finished*] as it sore fatigues me.

What was Ellison's job like?

- How many hours did she work a day?
- How heavy were her tubs of coal?
- What happened if she did not do enough work?

Chimney sweeps sent small boys up twisting chimneys to sweep them. The boys got lung diseases and sometimes fell. A law banned children from chimney sweeping in 1875.

New laws

After these reports, the government passed a Mines **Act** in 1842, which banned all girls and boys under the age of ten from working in mines. Another Act reduced children's working day in textile mills to ten hours. **Inspectors** visited mills to check the laws were obeyed.

7

ON THE FARM

Farmers struggled to make a living and needed children's earnings and help to support their families. Farm children always spent part of the year working, even when school became **compulsory**.

Seasonal work

Children went to school mainly in the autumn and winter when there was not much farm work to do. They stayed at home during hay making and harvest in the summer, when everyone lent a hand to get the crops in.

Harvest holidays

Schools tried to set summer holidays at harvest time. However, the harvest relied on the weather – if the harvest was late, children did not go to school until it was finished.

The men cut the hay with scythes. The women and older girls turned it with rakes to help it dry.

School **log book** entries

May 8
Poor attendance. Many children employed looking after cows and sheep.

June 3
Attendance scanty owing to children being wanted to assist with sheep shearing.

June 23
Many older children absent this week in consequence of hay making.

August 23
School breaks up today for the harvest holidays – for three weeks if harvest be over – otherwise for a month.

September 13
Attendance poor. It will not improve until the corn harvest is over.

November 7
Thin attendance, as so many children are potato digging.

Children's farm jobs throughout the year

Rattle used for bird scaring ▶

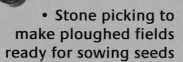

◀ Flagon for beer or cider

▼ Sheaf

(March–May) SPRING

- Stone picking to make ploughed fields ready for sowing seeds
- Weeding fields by hand
- Bird scaring
- Planting potatoes
- Minding sheep and pigs

SUMMER (June–August)

- Carrying refreshments to haymakers
- Vegetable and fruit picking
- Making bands for corn sheaves
- Gleaning (picking up leftover ears of wheat for using as animal feed or for grinding into flour for bread)

(December–March) WINTER

- Collecting windblown branches and twigs as extra firewood
- Gathering carrots, turnips and potatoes
- Cleaning turnips for animal feed
- Feeding cows and pigs inside

AUTUMN (September–November)

- Collecting acorns as food for pigs
- Picking potatoes
- Minding pigs
- Bird scaring for autumn sown crops
- Berry picking

Find out which of these farm jobs are still done today.

9

IN THE HOME

The most common job for girls, especially for those from the country, was as domestic (home) servants. The **census** of 1891 recorded 1.4 million female servants – more than 100,000 of them girls aged between ten and fourteen.

Servants' duties

Very rich households employed many servants, each with a specific job. Young girls started as scullerymaids, housemaids, nurse maids or laundry maids. They might progress to become cooks, housekeepers or nannies.

Nurse maids helped to look after young children.

Scullerymaids cleaned everything in the kitchen and helped to prepare food.

Housemaids dusted, swept, polished and scrubbed all the other rooms in the house.

Laundry maids washed and ironed clothes and bed linen.

Maids wore a uniform – a print dress for their morning work, and a black dress and a white apron and cap for greeting visitors in the afternoons.

HOUSEMAIDS BOX AND TRAY

An extract from *Mrs Beeton's Book of Household Management*, 1861

This is a list of what Mrs Beeton expected a maid to do before breakfast!
- Open the shutters and windows.
- Brush the range and light the fire.
- Clear away the ashes and clean the **hearth**.
- Polish the bright parts of the range.
- Put on the kettle.
- Sweep the dining room.
- Clean the grate and dust the furniture.
- Lay the table cloth for breakfast.
- Sweep the hall and shake the mats.
- Clean the doorstep.
- Polish the door knocker.
- Clean the boots.
- Bring the hot water **urn** into the dining room.
- Cook bacon, kidneys, fish, etc.

Which jobs still need doing in houses today?

Maid of all work

Most girls had a hard, lonely life as a maid of all work – the only servant in a house. They got up at 6am and often worked until midnight. They were badly paid and had little time off, but they were usually well fed. All their work was done by hand, because there were no electric machines for cooking, cleaning or washing.

Hot water and coal

Maids had a great deal of fetching and carrying to do. Hot water had to be heated on a coal-fired **range** and carried upstairs in cans for baths and washing. Coal had to be brought upstairs for the fires on every floor.

▼ Hot water can   ▼ Coal hod

COTTAGE INDUSTRIES

All over the country, young children worked in **cottage industries**, making things by hand.

Village handicrafts

In some villages, girls learned straw plaiting, or lace or glove making from the age of five or six. Either their mothers taught them or they went to classes, where teachers kept the children working hard, sometimes for ten hours a day.

Straw plaiting

At straw-plaiting schools, parents bought the children bundles of split straws. The children had to plait at least 20 metres of straw each day. The plaited straw was sold to hat makers for making into hats and bonnets.

Plaiting classes were held in local cottages. Sometimes as many as 30 children were crammed inside small rooms which had poor lighting, no heating and no fresh air.

Plaiting School

This girl is helping her mother, who is a box maker.

Homeworkers

In cities, many poor women took on work that could be done at home. They made paper bags, sweet wrappers, matchboxes, artificial flowers and Christmas crackers. Some wrapped up hairpins, sewed hooks and eyes onto display cards or hand painted greetings cards.

Nimble fingers

The workers were paid by the number of things they made, not by their time, so their children all helped. As one mother said, 'Of course, it's hard on the little ones, but their fingers are so quick – they that has the most of 'em is the best off.'

Extract from *Recollections of a School Attendance Officer* by John Reeves

They [*working children*] never played as children play, they never seemed to think as children. They were prematurely [*too soon*] old and the victims of awful cruelty.

SHOP BOYS

Victorian shops were small and run by their owners. Food shops, such as bakers, grocers and butchers, employed assistants and delivery boys to help them.

Delivery boys

There were no fridges in Victorian times, so people bought meat and groceries daily. Wealthy and middle-class people did not go shopping for food. Instead, delivery boys went to their houses collecting orders from the cook. Once the shopkeepers had made up the orders, the boys helped deliver the parcels to each house.

Milk delivery

By the middle of Victoria's reign, fresh milk was sent in churns from farms to towns by train. Boys helped delivery men take a churn on a cart around the streets. They measured out milk from metal cups into people's cans or jugs.

The butcher is giving his delivery boy orders for the day.

Milk delivery was done by horse cart like this, or by handcart, pulled by the delivery men.

Boys who worked in food shops wore long aprons over their clothes.

Newspaper advertisements for jobs in shops

BAKERS – Wanted Youth; good dough maker, moulder; to be generally useful; sober.

YOUTH (strong) – Wanted to help in baking and delivering; good character required.

YOUNG GIRL – Wanted to assist in house and shop; neat appearance and teachable.

BUTCHERS – Wanted; strong respectable country Youth as **Apprentice** to above **trade**.

Shop life

Young boys were used as 'barkers'. They stood outside shops, shouting out prices and praising the goods on sale. The shop assistants lived above the shop and worked hard. Shops were open every weekday until 10pm and on Saturdays until midnight. The assistants were not allowed to sit down and always had to look clean and neat to give customers a good impression.

What qualities did shopkeepers look for in their assistants?

15

STREET SELLERS

▲ Matchgirl

Children from very poor families and homeless orphans often became street sellers. They mainly sold small, cheap, useful, everyday things.

Tiring work

Children as young as six went out selling. They did not dare go home until they had earned enough money for the day. They worked long hours, often up to midnight, in all weathers, sometimes seven days a week.

An interview with a flower seller from Henry Mayhew's *London's Labour and the London Poor*

I have no relation in the world. I met a young woman in the street... who advised me to take up flower selling, as I could get nothing else to do. She showed me to market with her and showed me how to bargain with the salesman for flowers. At first when I went out to sell, I felt so ashamed I could not ask anyone else to buy of me.

- Why did this girl start selling flowers?
- Why might she have felt ashamed?

Girls sold bunches of flowers, watercress and lavender, or oranges.

Newsboys

Boys sold newspapers on the street. At a time when there was no television or radio, newspapers were printed three times a day to give people the latest news. The bigger the story – such as a murder, a football match or a flood – the more newspapers the boys sold.

▲ Newsboys

Henry Mayhew, a journalist, discovered children selling things like these on the street.

▲ Clothes pegs

▲ Steel pen

▲ Nutmeg grater

Costerboys

Costermongers, who sold fruit and vegetables from barrows, employed boys to shout out prices in their loud, shrill voices. The boys also helped to pull the barrows from street to street.

▲ Costerboy

GUTTERSNIPES

In big towns, poor and homeless boys, known as guttersnipes or street urchins, did all sorts of odd jobs to scratch a living.

Anything for a penny

Boys carried luggage to and from train stations, delivered parcels or ran messages. They held horses while their owners went into shops or visited houses. Some were link-boys, who lit the way with flaming torches for people out late at night.

This cartoon shows how desperate boys fought to get a horse cab for a waiting gentleman.

Passers by gave small change to boys who performed acrobatics, played music or sang on street corners.

Link-boys led people through the dense fogs that often shrouded big cities.

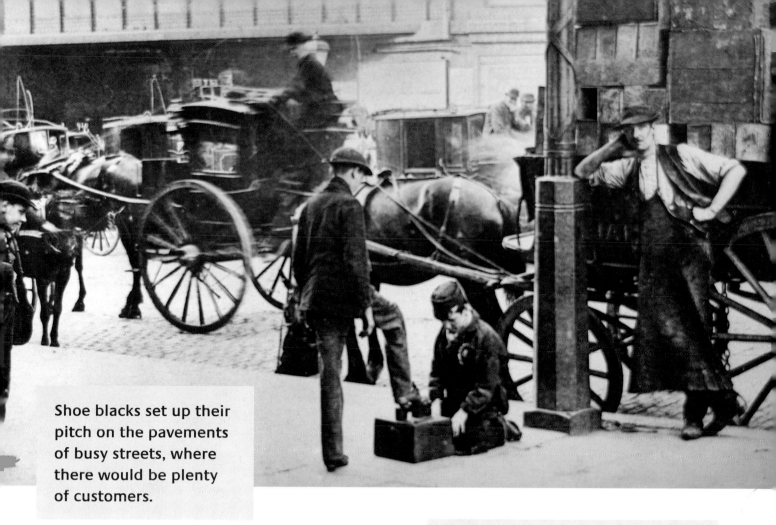

Shoe blacks set up their pitch on the pavements of busy streets, where there would be plenty of customers.

Shoe blacks

Some boys had more regular work. In 1851, the Earl of Shaftesbury set up the London Shoe Black Brigade to help children who shined shoes. The boys were given a uniform – a cap, an apron and a coloured jacket to show the area where they worked. In the evenings, they went to a **Ragged School** where they learned to read and write.

Crossing sweepers

Boys also worked at road junctions as crossing sweepers. Each one had a particular spot where he worked.

Rich people paid crossing sweepers to sweep away mud and horse dung, so that their polished shoes and long skirts would not get dirty.

SCAVENGERS

The poorest children of all **scavenged** for rubbish. They collected anything that could be resold and reused.

▲ Rat poison bottle

Useful finds

Scavengers in the street were known as pickers-up. Their finds included bones, pieces of string, old iron, scraps of paper, broken crockery, empty tins, buttons, wire, pieces of wood, boot heels, medicine and other bottles, and damaged milk cans and saucepans.

Earnings

Many pickers-up were homeless. They spent the money they earned on a cheap lodging-house, bread and tea.

The children sorted their finds and sold them to specialist dealers or on a market stall.

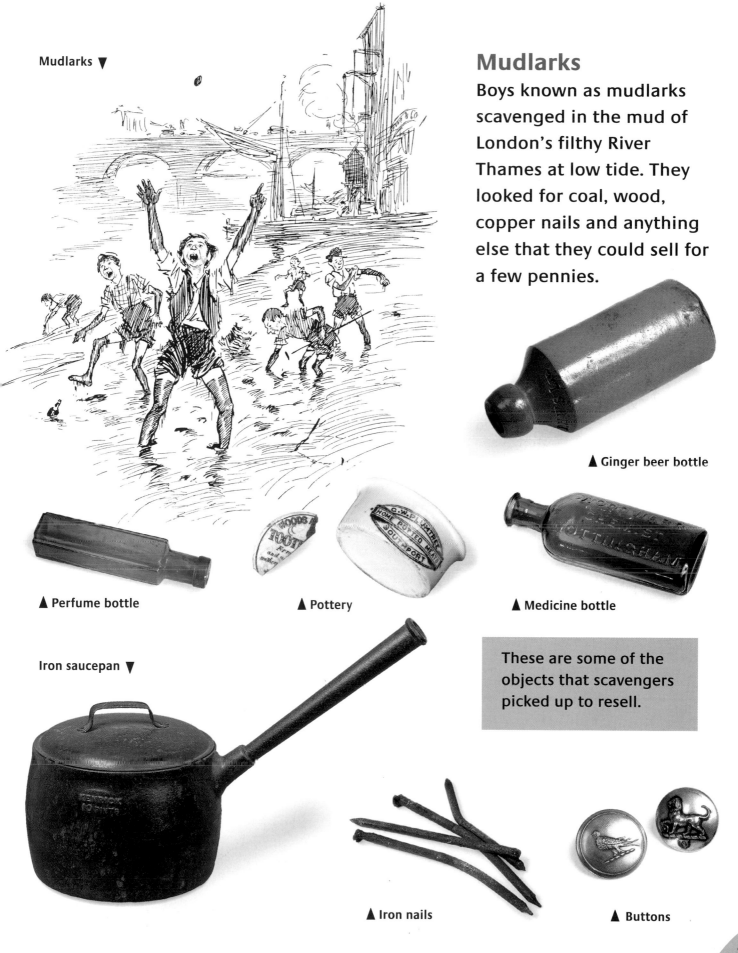

Mudlarks

Boys known as mudlarks scavenged in the mud of London's filthy River Thames at low tide. They looked for coal, wood, copper nails and anything else that they could sell for a few pennies.

▲ Ginger beer bottle

▲ Perfume bottle

▲ Pottery

▲ Medicine bottle

Mudlarks ▼

These are some of the objects that scavengers picked up to resell.

Iron saucepan ▼

▲ Iron nails

▲ Buttons

HELPING CHILDREN

Many Victorians became very worried about children who had no families, homes or regular work, and who were often forced to beg or steal to survive.

Schools and refuges

In large towns, Ragged Schools were set up to teach poor children for free. These often provided meals and clothing as well as lessons. Wealthy people funded refuges where orphans could live and learn 'an honest trade'.

The boys at this school learned to sew, so they had a chance to become tailors when they grew up.

Girls of different ages lived together in the 50 cottages of the Village Home, looked after by a 'mother'.

Dr Barnado

Thomas Barnado was a doctor who lived and worked in the poor East End of London. He was horrified to discover homeless children sleeping on roofs, huddled against chimneys to keep warm.

A home for girls

Barnado opened homes for these children, including a Village Home for Girls. The girls were trained to be servants. On their 13th birthday, they left to work. The best pupils were given a maid's uniform to take with them.

23

SCHOOLS

By the end of Queen Victoria's reign, there had been many changes, including schooling, that improved the chances in life for children.

Hundreds of new schools were built after 1870 – especially big ones like this in cities.

Forced to school

After 1880, children had to go to school by law. Parents had to pay, until schooling was made free in 1891, so many poor children were kept away from school. Attendance officers went in search of children who were working or helping at home. Parents could be fined if their children missed school. By 1900, most children were regular pupils.

Find out what jobs, if any, children are allowed to do today.

- At what age can children start doing paid work?
- How many hours a day are they allowed to work?

Half-timers

Gradually, it became more difficult for children to work full-time, although many still worked before and after school. In mills, many girls were half-timers. This meant they worked at the mill for half the day and went to school for the rest of the day. The children were often so tired from their work that they found it hard to concentrate on lessons and even fell asleep.

Learning a trade

Older boys often spent their last year at school learning a trade, such as tailoring, printing, shoe making, gardening or carpentry.

▲ A half-timer in a cotton mill

These boys are learning how to make men's suits.

FINDING OUT MORE

Do your own research to find out more about Victorian working children, the places they worked and the people who helped them.

▲ Mill workers in Manchester in 1865

Children's work

The work that Victorian children did varied according to where they lived and whether they lived in a town or the country. Find out what work Victorian children did in your local area.

People who helped

Find out about the lives of these people who helped to improve children's lives.

Dr Thomas Barnado (1845–1905)

www.barnados.org.uk

Robert Owen (1771–1858)

www.robert-owen.com

www.newlanark.org

Lord Ashley, from 1851 the Earl of Shaftesbury (1805–1885)

www.spartacus.school.net.co.uk/IRchild.htm

Part of a speech made by Lord Ashley to Parliament in 1840

A humble address be presented to her Majesty, praying that her Majesty will be graciously pleased to direct an inquiry... in the various branches of trade and manufacture in which numbers of children work together... and to collect information as to the ages at which they are employed, the numbers of hours they are engaged in work, the times allowed each day for meals and as to the actual state, condition and treatment of such children and as to the effect of such employment, both with regard to their morals and to their health.

Looking at buildings

Some Victorian mills are still standing, but they are no longer in use as mills. They either house other types of businesses or have been converted into museums, offices or homes.

Spotting clues

- Many old mills and factories are huge, multi-storeyed buildings.
- They usually have many large windows.
- The first mills were built on the banks of rivers or canals. Waterwheels provided power for the machines.
- Later, machines were powered by steam. Burning coal heated the water. Tall chimneys let the smoke escape.

Armley Mill in Leeds was once the largest woollen mill in the world. It is now an industrial museum where you can see working spinning, carding and weaving machines, and learn about the work that adults and children did.

TIMELINE

1837 Victoria came to the throne.

1840s

1842 A Mines Act banned boys under the age of ten and all girls and women from working in mines.

1844 A law was passed saying that factory machinery had to be guarded.

1847 The Ten Hours Act reduced the working day in mills for children to ten hours a day.

1870s

1870 Government-run Board Schools were set up for children under the age of ten.

1871 Easter Monday, Whit Monday, the last Monday in August and 26 December were made **Bank Holidays.**

1872 Girls were banned from working in brickyards.

1874 A Factory Act raised the minimum working age to nine years.

1875 Young boys were banned from working as chimney sweeps.

1890s

1891 A Factory Act raised the minimum working age to 11.

1891 Schooling was made free.

1892 The Shop Hours Act that limited working hours for under 18s was strengthened and enforced by inspectors.

1893 The school leaving age was raised to 11.

1850s

1857 The Industrial Schools Act allowed schools to be set up for neglected and homeless children who might turn to crime.

1860s

1867 The Workshop Act banned children under the age of eight from working in any factory or workshop.

1867 A Factory Act forbade children, young people and women from working on Sundays.

1880s

1880 Schooling for children between the ages of five and ten was made compulsory.

1886 A Shops Hours Act limited working hours of people under 18 to 74 hours a week.

1887 Queen Victoria's Golden Jubilee (50 years on the throne) took place.

1887 Queen Victoria medals were introduced to encourage perfect attendance at school.

1900s

1894 The Prevention of Cruelty to Children Act banned children under 11 from performing or selling things in the street.

1897 Queen Victoria's Diamond Jubilee (60 years on the throne) took place.

1899 The school leaving age was raised to 12.

1901 Queen Victoria died.

GLOSSARY

Act a piece of law

apprentice a person learning a skill from someone who is already doing it

Bank Holidays several weekdays (often Mondays) in the year when banks, shops and factories are officially shut

census a count of people living in a country. The census started in Britain in 1801 and has been taken every ten years (except 1941)

commissioner a person appointed to do a specific task – such as visit factories to check working conditions

compulsory must be done

cottage industry work that people do in their own homes, often using their own tools and equipment

hearth the floor of a fireplace

inhale to breathe in

inspector someone whose job it is to visit a place, such as a factory or school, to make sure it is run properly

law a rule made by Parliament that everyone must obey

log book a school diary in which the head teacher filled in details of what happened at school each day

orphan a child whose parents are both dead

Parliament the place where elected MPs (Members of Parliament) meet to discuss and make laws for the country

Ragged School a free school for the very poorest children

range a kitchen stove built into the fireplace

scavenge to search amongst rubbish for things that can be used or eaten

textile cloth

trade a job that needs skill and training

urn a large metal container with a tap, used for heating water

PLACES TO VISIT

All the places below have exhibitions related to Victorian children at work. Some are displayed in restored factories, mills or farms. At some places, you can go down a coal mine or up a chimney.

Acton Scott Historic Working Museum
Wenlock Lodge, Church Stretton, Shropshire SY6 6QN
www.shropshireonline.gov.uk/museums.nsf

Armley Mills Industrial Museum
Canal Road, Armley, Leeds LS12 2QF
www.leeds.gov.uk/armleymills

Beamish: North of England Open Air Museum
Beamish, County Durham DH9 0RG
www.beamish.org.uk

Big Pit: National Mining Museum (Wales)
Blaenafon, Gwent, Wales NP4 9XP
www.nmgw.ac.uk/bigpit

The Black Country Living Museum
Tipton Road, Dudley, West Midlands DY1 4SQ
www.bclm.co.uk

Bradford Industrial Museum
Moorside Road, Bradford, W. Yorkshire BD2 3HP
www.bradfordmuseums.org/bim/bim_main.htm

Brewhouse Yard Museum
Castle Boulevard, Nottingham NG7 1FB
www.nottinghamcity.gov.uk/sitemap/brewhouse_yard

Erddig
Wrexham LL13 0YT
www.nationaltrust.org.uk

Ironbridge Gorge Museums
Ironbridge, Telford, Shropshire TF8 7AW
www.ironbridge.org.uk

Macclesfield Heritage Centre
Roe Street, Macclesfield, Cheshire SK11 6UT
www.silk-macclesfield.org

Museum of English Rural Life
Redlands Road, Reading, Berkshire RG1 5EX
www.reading.ac.uk/Instits/im

Museum of London
London Wall, London EC2Y 5HN
www.museumoflondon.org.uk

Museum of Science and Industry in Manchester
Liverpool Road, Castlefield, Manchester M3 4FP
www.msim.org.uk

National Coal Mining Museum for England
Caphouse Colliery, New Road, Overton, Wakefield, West Yorkshire WF4 4RH
www.ncm.org.uk

New Lanark World Heritage Site
South Lanarkshire, Scotland ML11 9DB
www.newlanark.org

Quarry Bank Mill
Styal, Cheshire SK9 4LA
www.quarrybankmill.org.uk

St Fagans National History Museum (Wales)
St Fagans, Cardiff CF5 6XB
www.nmgw.ac.uk/stfagans

Shugborough Historic Estate
Milford, near Stafford ST17 0XB
www.shugborough.org.uk

Sudbury Hall – the National Trust Museum of Childhood
Sudbury, Ashbourne, Derbyshire DE6 5HT
www.nationaltrust.org.uk

Ulster Folk and Transport Museum
Cultra, Holywood, County Down, N. Ireland BT18 0EU
www.uftm.org.uk

Weald and Downland Museum
Singleton, Sussex PO18 0EU
www.wealddown.co.uk

Wigan Pier Heritage Centre
Wigan, Lancashire WN3 4EU
www.destinationwigan.com

INDEX

These are the lists of contents for each title in *A Victorian Childhood*: